Not There – Here

Also by Andrew Taylor

Silo (The Red Ceilings Press, 2021)
Adrian Henri: A Critical Reading (Greenwich Exchange, 2019)
Lowdeine Chronicles (with Nick Power, erbacce-press, 2019)
at first it felt like flying (with Charlie Baylis, Indigo Dreams, 2019)
Aire (The Red Ceilings Press, 2018)
15.11.13. – 5.2.14 (Stranger Press, 2018)
The 140's (Leafe Press, 2018)
March (Shearsman Books, 2017)
Liverpool Warehousing Co. Ltd. (zimZalla, 2016)
Airvault (Oystercatcher, 2016)
Future Dust (Original Plus, 2015)
Radio Mast Horizon (Shearsman Books, 2013)
Comfort and Joy (Ten Pages Press, 2011)
The Lights Will Inspire You (Full of Crow Press, 2011)
The Sound of Light Aircraft (Knives Forks and Spoons Press, 2010)
The Metaphysics of a Vegetarian Supper (Differentia Press, 2009)
And the Weary Will Rest (Sunnyoutside Press, 2008)
Poetry and Skin Cream (erbacce-press, 2004 and 2007)
Temporary Residence (erbacce-press, 2007)
Cathedral Poems (Paula Brown Publishing, 2005)

Andrew Taylor

Not There – Here

Shearsman Books

First published in the United Kingdom in 2021 by
Shearsman Books
PO Box 4239
Swindon
SN3 9FN

Shearsman Books Ltd Registered Office
30–31 St. James Place, Mangotsfield, Bristol BS16 9JB
(this address not for correspondence)

www.shearsman.com

ISBN 978-1-84861-787-2

Contents

I   There

II   Here

For Rachel Smith

Silence per se *is of course, non-existent.*
— Peter Gidal

40 years ago, we were living (and dreaming) of the future. 40 years later, we're living and dreaming of the past. We were living our best days and didn't even know it.
— globalturfwar

I

THERE

Twelve

Last night you had the strangest dream
you sailed in a little rowing boat to China

to look for me & I said 'I have to get
my laundry washed & nothing is going

to stop me nothing's going to break my stride I've got to
        keep moving'

So I do I keep moving walking the hill
delivering bread & poetry the basket

is empty clothes washed & noodles
are simmering in the pan

September Fields

Through hedgerow gaps between trees
an undulation perhaps it's to do with

colour a golden calm sets in at summer's
end spiders come in from cooling night air

heating is entertained flowers last through
though the evenings don't gather wood

like windfalls essential in preparation
warming like a playing angel

in candlelight shadows alter with draughts
that rise through polished floorboards

kicking fallen leaves in tyre tracks
those who have gone before somehow remain

as gouges in earth and remaining leaves
on trees evergreens that battle winter

Gravy

The jeans are soaked in gravy
arranging the towels

on their rail there is that smell
not of laundry but of gravy

the dust from the drill settles
in the most awkward of places

under the window resembles a
hardware store

the treacle porter tastes of treacle
and darkens the glass

at night there is the feeling
of being at sea even though

the bed is anchored firmly
to the first floor

Yard Work

for Peter Hughes

Bang the tin out
     repair
photograph
       with a pedal

Log cabin
     in the woods
every country has coffee

Pull the can
     get in the fields
every patch a memory

Every camp
      needs a good fire
chopper and bossman

Bits of dust
      smudges of slip
start the eggshell seeds

Wood shovel
     salt repeat
this is a process

Tempelhof

the quiet days
   between Christmas
and New Year

Not working
    not celebrating

Liner notes
an excerpt
   London Records (556 113-2) 1999

...all Ma's and Da's
the fella who sorted out Mick's PRS on Christmas Eve,
Eddie and the boys at Cash Converters, Dr Detox from
Stapleford, Hugo, Youth man

The fact that it gets
dark so early

feels
like jet lag

Snowcave melting in Tempelhof

There is an increased patience
for cooking
and making
the apartment cosy

The sheen of a new shirt
wear for days
remove before eating

coloured paper chain
plant drape

ensure to draw
    yourself
out of the sadness

[Acknowledgements to Ronnie Hughes; a sense of place blog, MIDIgrrrl, Roary Yum/ClintonLevy]

Above there are three helicopters

As we sit among
riverside sculpture,

barges shift
containers. Inside

a gallery space,
the M53 appears

quiet in the dark,
traffic-less.

A jib shifts silently
above the station.

Let's not live in
fragments, there's

too much connectivity
let's learn to tango.

Polaroid

Thirty years
an instant

like a developing Polaroid
you eventually
appear

as though in disguise

hunt through dates
seek evidence

so come on climb in

It is now a shift
a recognition

Real English Tea

Natalie said they made
      Billy a saint

Turnbull said he drank
      more tea than Dr Johnson

Timely from Thurston
      and Chelsea Light Moving

Glass and Reich as
      removers

on 23rd Street I bet it was
      freshly roasted

an amphetamine sonnet for
      on-the-loose lovers

take the single estate
      from the flask on the verge

Also known as Walden

for, and i.m. Jonas Mekas

In New York
         it was still winter

but the wind was full of spring

Barbara planting flower seeds
on the windowsill

apple blossoms

Photograph the dust falling
on the city
on the windows
on the books

everywhere

I thought of home

The girl with the bicycle
and blue shirt
Diane in Central Park
touching grass with her foot

In front of the church
                 the wedding party
New York hotel
(Fifth Ave & 62nd St.) Sept. 18, 1965

A small animal
in the dark branches
of night

Flowers and street noise

September
  Autumn came with wind and gold

Street works
crossing the park looking at autumn

Coal deliverer
camera clicks
a black coal worker unloading a coal truck

Wet city streets
lights at night

  daytime snow scenes
in the park

window cleaner on Columbus Ave.

Deep of winter
sick in bed looking at the window
necktie
the friend Cat

Winter scene
Amy stops for coffee

Street works
Peace March at night

Late winter slush

People moving across the woods
blown by wind

end station
   coffee
warming up

END OF REEL THREE

Working table
         drinking coffee

On the melting porch
         Jane cleans the roof

suddenly it looked like spring

GULF COAST UNDERGROUND IN SPRING FEVER

Sunrise on way back
   to New York
New Jersey skyline
   smokestacks
chimneys

soon after that
         came Autumn

trees and park at the university

branches in wind
a brook in autumn woods

Chelsea Hotel
                  the window
                  the street
newspaper man
on 23rd St & 7th Ave corner

winter scene

deep of Winter
                        snow fight on Bleecker St

picketing in snow and cold
heavy with rucksacks and things

Sunday morning

I thought of home

Metal Box

White paintings came first;
my silent piece came later —*John Cage*

I

Attached by rope
history painting
changing constantly

Regretful paint drips
wishes to be seen
act between the two

Plan lay out stretcher
floor match markings
join monumental gravity

II

Below skin soil dirt
axe shank stickered
air flow flick lighter orange

Break dusk down
core candlelight
piano processed sounds

coldness stagnant dock
beyond Belfast boat
strings tidal stab

The Holy Fold

Sweeping gathering leaves
in early autumn

Walking footpaths retracing childhood
ensuring the Fold's history is told

Shovelling salting paths
after sudden snowfall

lodging memory under department
store stairs to be excavated on return

Lighting a fire in a house
without central heating

Cereal giver news gatherer
village life fade meal deliverer

Chopping bagging wood
for a smokeless zone home

Vintage square photographs
analogue architecture light within

Woolfox

No! It's not spring
      full salt barn
roadside

Useless depot
pre-dawn birdsong

Blue bucket of Gold
     refrain
the sound of
    a windswept shore

inland the A1 winds its way
North
     Hit it!

River

The ultimate condition of everything is *river:*
light, mass, form —Iain Sinclair

there is a river forever flowing forever changing,
there is a river forever going places —R.O.C

We are in constant flow
noise and smells gather at dawn
spread evenly

Beyond the wall weeds grow in cracks
like thick clothes on a warm day
this is wrong

Acoustic string combination rolls
in on the tide gathers momentum
before the evening silence

Warehouses and inclines in built
guidance system demolished streets
take with them more than mortar

Scars deeper than paper cuts avoid
the cliché of ink work until
your arms ache

What sounds like a foghorn is at play
like when we

slept on the floor during
The Great Storm of 1987

There is a beautiful sun over the river

Analogue

weekend reading
ink stains
load a
memory bottle

by treading steps
annually
quiet wisdom

of the wild
and general
pace

of walking
through streets
with cast iron
signs

rusted moulded
letters

birdsong dust
in cobblestone tracks
layered history

Star Locks

Boarded up
two-week roses company
horizontal weather

curtains back sodium flash
watch for slower fall

Rails shine above white
aside from overnight rust

Look on the estate from the turret
forget about the broken

Pray for the dead
pray for me

Technology is not secure

Peeled paint reveals layers of age
the longer it's left

Pacing Call

Like glass in a turned field
it is recognition of shift

I prefer Tarmac in re-laid
car parks at twilight

with the evening calls of birds
the sharing of information

becomes priority

Sycamore Street

Seek the operator a night
      in an empty house
before the cellular aged miracle

number not yet registered
or located in directory

She feels for the tilting
postbox

Autumn song of the blackbird
          pre-Dawn
like pips

analogue as a Market & Fairs
licence

after shift communication
crumble of pharmacy bag
      new advice for drivers

order phone box coffee
spot *the* Paul Smith
      ask for an apron

[051 547 922 521]

Marker flags placed
party line cleared

mode telecom
    Telex fax

green paint for rural areas
poetry for New Year's Day
curl of steam from a coffee cup

Creosote poles
          wires stripped
salvaged fir
                    you were going through
the photos on your phone

The room's echo slows
the line crackle   from Paris
                    1988
feeding francs into the box
on Boulevard St Germain

call Sylvia tell her she
can collect us in the morning

Star Form

for Flo Fflach

Anyone else?
      two punnets of strawberries
a pound now

Rural psychedelica
        dreaming hill
Ultrahigh frequency

Rail replacement bus

A blackbird sings

May the sea and light wash
      & illuminate us
recycled green heart

Rag-jack for false Oxslip
      nothingness blossom
textile solid precipitation

at times lovely weather
      for chasing sheep

Edge Seed

After Richard Skelton

edge seed
they will place   and make outwards
dying
outwards dying
after remnants
                       (rowan)
the moorland
go heart and will for it in time
moorland
        go reach richer place
make others
will
    make to the trees and the heart

and make the edge bracken
                   thriving to follow moorland
go oak seed
                     (pine)
It's bracken and broom
they (broom)
  the moorland unhindered
nature remake again
let bare outwards
dying trees and after

Sitting with Alex Katz

Pansies and *Tulips* outside a Ferry is battling the tide it is a
Saturday in March in Liverpool and a girl in DM boots stares
longingly at *Full Moon 1988* it could have been us at the gallery
opening in 1988 when it all began you in Liberty Print me in
501s

    for Nic

*

Through these tunnels for the thousandth time or more
sparks arc walls light for a second trace of 126 one over seven
105 departure point smudged in light rain gate to connecting
platform open signal free red leaks through from stop point
forecast amber warning third rail freeze

*

Those trips are getting better and better. They are. The
circuitous route shines. The weather is on the turn. Next time,
the Carhartt will appear. The Ikon lift, sings. It's just the way it
is. Though it appears clear, it isn't: 2326 XGC 663 XGC 426
CP 413 C & 7554 CP let's mark it.

*

Though the cut is less oily it is no less inviting daybreak over
the former Royal Mail sorting office waiting on the bridge for
the movement of barges what degree of angle they'll take tea for
two at the table with the blue cloth it's about checking people
are ok & listening

*

Fit the bones reward collars that have been scrubbed clean.
Names hidden from view, an appropriate side shift. Like
hidden photographs between pages as the words are read aloud,
it is the knowing, the travelling and buying of French bread at
Sunday markets with the words etched.

Sidings

i.m. John James

Sunday morning kettle sings
pitch perfect
the first pot waits to be made
Rachel reading behind
the stacks
of the Poetry Library
In a garage in north Liverpool
an axe
slowly rusts awaiting attention
Weetabix for supper a
curious defect
in the hunt for cream
A couple in The Punter
before the last train home

Intermodal

Moody
sidings
turn to
light

Heavy
pap
breakfast
time

Prior to
demolition
unfurl
to find

love
there is
no harbour
here

the sea
is unkind
to
trespassers

With the Tide

Sound of blind
            rattle
afternoon into early evening sky

clearing
            replicated
white of spots
blue of background

rooftops
            spread   green   horizon

with the tide comes the change

lavender blackbird spins

tambourine shakes in sequence

            tea and thirteen senses
blue top milk

no use for cardboard
                  rip things up!

vintage digitised
Sam streamed
                  dance of the summer
Seeking his peaches to share

It is summer after all

[thanks to Rachel Smith]

British Salt

for Robert Sheppard at 60

Not soup not again
The use of staples publication from SW17

21 shutters 21 shelters
The home which functions as your second skull

Re-working the work: pausing for breath

Zayneb dresses like Leila Khalid
                    Fox Spotlights

Norwich March 1975 something about
homecoming

Lee Harwood above a pub, Liverpool March
21st 2014

Cut back to seafront / river misty morning / misty morning
ship leaving port / bay

A birthday correspondence 21st March 2015 07.26

What once belonged to poetry has been stolen

the white shirted figure in the top right window in L18
is not eating soup

Twelve hours in between a snowdrop walk manufactured pictorial hall footprint mapped rent the cabin for £25 day starts 5.45 a.m. with song arguably ends at 5.45 p.m. a version of the same song analogue treatment at its best set the room for great white spaces & valve silence

i.m. Mark Hollis

*

Long White Split Tin strip then wrap cables prepare for transportation A50 neon spray Diesel engine tick *meet at the bakery like we usually do* waterfront rendezvous collar turned shoes scuffed blast of river colour amidst courtyard grey bread brown paper wrap a traditional bake

*

Filtered rose light of dawn awaits the stretching of perennial sowthistle. You only know a lane by repeatedly walking amongst its dust. Vine leaf dangles on spider web strand, dances to the shift in breeze. Later, ivy leaf joins in to a different tune: repetitive blackbird song.

*

A slight cough left channel. The scaling back of wrists, the beginning of semi-circular blackness. A basic formula masked by glitch, becomes cacophonous. The need to stretch outside of the zone, with immersive travel & isolation, a mild obsession to avoid the city & temptation.

*

Train composition poster line up arranged fireworks spark Le Pont *don't fall asleep with wet hair* skim pebbles Polaroid sidewalk overcoat shelter radio's on the blink *maybe just one more coffee by the fire* before we enter tunnels spot tags track clatter ball bearing can rattle

Larch

The larch has been felled
                        Phytophthora ramorum

let's drive the different route 17 miles
cattle grids
            empty feedbags
            strung like scarecrows

Railway at times runs parallel
ballast plumb line straight

Our single track
                        Passing place

Signal stagnant
            inactivity

signpost navigation GPS
                        unnamed road

follow the quietness
valley empty   it looks like a bomb's gone off

toward the estate there is cover
thirty five years ago
we took this drive   tracks remain

for supplies
milk bread
tea

the forest is weak it is halved
    the lochs become visible
their tracks evident

above the grey house
commands

Gibraltar

You may see monkeys
or dancing shadows
like at the Empire Theatre
April 26th 1981

The Long Days Tour
camouflage left in
storage final port
of call

tainted blood often
creates an impending
sense of doom
so does parting

Shred

Port air carries across rooftops
you busy with loft work
& tradition electrical tape
sticking of spines

Among the flowers a solitary bee
sketched with precision
carried in a manuscript
across four cities

Collect tickets to be archived
in a shoebox regardless
of journeys take a knife
to 10 year-old statements

as silk strands catch the light
before the closing of the hatch

Jandek

i.m. Tom Raworth

Where can we go
when we retire?
which hold me
down by my head?

experience perhaps
shooting along (alone)
stockings because the word means
what comes to mind
and turn
time: art is beamed to
those antenna education
should tune
rumours of the present (any present)
then *deja vu* is a true
doppler effect

Even the colour film appears to be black and white

we are adrift
   with machines
& determined uses

development of
   secret commodities
& bogus anniversaries

paint rails white or better
still buy higher grade steel
& be prepared to forecast

Obsessed by its own culture
it can't see what inner city
people's minds might be

Late editions fail
    to impress peddling
guff from kiosks

jackets are fastened
    in preparation
freak weather on the continent

freak privilege & charity
    status the officials believe
solely in bin bags

Nocturnal Interludes

When you are awake
we are awake

Step into a story book
through the abbey gates

save on travel spend on
memories enjoy a magical

Christmas month in France
festive fries £2.39

Late night trains evenings out
travel the loop

Market Street fairy lights
2nd Not in Service

Kev said the station at night
was really dodgy

Of Ploughland

In a Bogart movie
platform

Stoney mountain
side
moments

Of ploughland half weary England

II

HERE

En France et en Europe

The clack of oiled bubbles
blue sea horses
     outside the water closet

This bunting will remain
for 10 days
     until the airport trip

Milk churn 239 on guard
outside the re-rendered
     doorway

The vine has blight the pepper
is low take the rock
     to lock the shutter in place

the quality of aluminium
is second to none
     it helps the taste

Coated dust ceiling window
blue of pre-dusk swifts
     break into the plain

     *

Fizz of fly morning fighting
hornets tea drinking routine
     gravel footsteps

sore and weary cut back
along the fence gap blister
        souvenir shower

of stone gate closed coated
in grey matching rare cloud
        relief of shade

Make dust coat the rear window
trace night activity
        En France et en Europe

With the rain comes bunting
removal a certain freshness
        across the lanes

aged beams footsteps on
plasterboard teen daze rework
        a perfect fit

Moncontour

On the terrace the Slovakian
waitress speaks English

The net is made of concrete
the slide is yellow and green

Kenkō would appreciate the shade
thrown by the poplars

a light aircraft circles the lake
the lip salve is melting

The Trowels are Wrapped in Bubble Wrap

tied by a blue elastic band
for transportation
forgotten in an outside pocket
like a removed movie snippet

from an archived recording scrub
the hand clean of black ink

cut to point a 60's gable end
25 years after building
travel lightly two backpacks
600 miles south before departure
unclip the battery oil under nails
tag-lined welcome to north station
Tox spotting underground shortening
gaps across the city

Kidman

lookalike smiles
the first offering of the day

it's 16.25 in Montparnasse
the travelator is broken
Orange priority tag shifts
waiting room makeover
light catches gold dances on
a pillar like *Seahorses on Broadway*
it's 17.21 in Montparnasse
& TGV 8389 departs on time
this second city petite moineau
spires & towers

recognisable routes track curves
& date stamps

Poem beginning with a line of John James

As August counts itself out
so the percentage plummets

reading pamphlets avec pastis
as is to expected

Words out of Time 'The Collect Gallery crammed with poets' p.43

Down to the lake for birding
stench of beached dead carp

Kenny trains the scope on the island
sunlight on the water

there is a poem in that
no, there is a poem in that

The respite of a rest area
temperature drops at midnight

Carried sandwiches foil & plastic
wrapped evening before

some kind of souvenir bread
like bread bought from a post office

Treated like a treat some things taste
better away from home

Mattresses floored a camp
shutters shut this is France after all

Reading Robert Sheppard in La Chaussée

Timely meeting before departure
    Fly in the Loaf
same seats

at the bar as last year
    we raise
a glass to Lee and talk about his

reading at the Cali
       where he wished
me happy birthday and wrote it

in his *Collected Poems*

A gift 'Words out of Time'
snuck in an envelope
the folded Best Wishes for 2009

text image by Patricia
'There can never be too much joy' —Greenbank Park 2006

Gulls crossed out
    hand annotation
Sea birds

Liverpool Gin in The Belvedere
the city rain soaked

Down hill
    colour neon splash
Bold St
    Central 16 minutes

I mourn the pool
　　　　　It's not
easy to escape

It's never easy to leave

Reclaim Victorialand

There is no exclusivity
it is timeless
wait for Liz to project

she belongs here now
just like Flying Saucer Attack
and the *Instrumentals 2015*

it becomes a part
as much as the dust
from the track

or the sunset beyond

TGV 8382

Sunflowers bow
row after row

season seems
hardly done

time for Autumn
reflections

so soon?

Easter Piano

for Nick Power

Wish I was on the whiskey
where you are
It's freezing here

It's Canadian
without ice

the pegs remain on the line

Marx 'The Civil War in France'
popular historical circumstances

Easter piano
rural France

Boxes unearthed
glass survived the trip

Softness of keys
sustain

Easter everywhere

8.01

Individual colours
fade

Top road
diesel engine

breaks through

Grasses fence weave
an atmospheric hue

a beautiful drift

19.05

gate   closure

Profil Aromatique

Metro flash
        a poem in a fax
telecommunication
& affidavits

leave the chateau on the 9.18

follow the scales
        melody to form
magnetics
& tape

return from Gare de l'Est on the 6.23

with flea market vinyl
vocal sourced & replicated

Bon

Touché de Tea

gather roundels
     fresh bakery
bread strong black

the basics of a European
   breakfast

International editions
   newspapers
arrive on the early train
like the stage

take the fast train
to Paris

take tea in standard
it's the English way

As soon as you leave the bed is stripped. Morning routine becomes quieter, the grinding of coffee beans once more becomes a solo activity. Thirty-year old compositions play in a different room. Outside, between pieces, a flap of wings and the rushed scamper for berries & grain.

*

Explain to Andrew the process it's not as grey as expected it could almost be summer aside from the temperature (a clear 30 degrees cooler than August) very light blue 283 C 536 C pale blue black 3 C in rear shadow facing the field remnants of rain on the worn tarmacked lane

*

In search of week-old tyre tracks the lane appears different of course it isn't, it's merely the light. The drift of ribbon on a homemade courtyard wreath, frost fading slowly. Behind the rear wall of the chateau, the brook runs fast, marked by three stakes and faded blue twine.

*

Instrumentals #1 fade in #2 processed picking #3 rolling waves slow crash toward melody #4 tape start #5 shorter melody #6 jet take off #7 oxidisation #8 noticeably guitar #9 soaring motif #10 crickets #11 of itself #12 indistinguishable #13 canal bank #14 motorway #15 statement

Juno

skirts around the tomato plants
before pinching out   Kevin showed
her the way

On the gravel drive a shape is left
when a car departs   It's easy to
count individual stones

Juno plays the stereo loudly
she says it helps   the tomatoes
especially when it rains

Jacaranda

Cosy & casual   origins in coffee
the espresso machine was an innovation

Beans on toast & Coca-Cola as payment

south of the equator   carpet seems
unnecessary 49 species to choose from

like lavender mist the eye is drawn to horizons

a cello melody   piano refrain
sequencing is a part like hand movement

Fog Couch

After sleep deprivation an amplified
sensitivity ride the market carousel

Sage when brushed releases its scent
brew Holiday Blend for the *Net & Ball* mug

A goods train leaves Canada Dock
spoon no. 142 is made of sycamore

A robin hops across a garden ash pile
apple wood stacked low lying mist

Market Street gravy simmers on the hob
Brassée dans le Nord depuis 1921

£1.35 International Air Mail franked stamp
two men wander around the harbour

Planes stack over south London
red lit city winter obscured sky view

Moss Wall

Year's end frost returns
French oak smoke
across winter sky
Painting in the cold just the job
for this time of year

Dampened forest piano
softness of omelette
slowly cooking
Blue soft edged light
a natural tinsel

Acknowledgements to Polly Atkin and Cliff Yates

Mistel Tan

After last leaf fall
 ground a white sheet
check pairing
 & count berries

Poem in two Spaces
after Alberto Giacometti

(Square)

cuckoo echo
a half second delay

(Square)

        pine needle
        pathway

the green field of folly
elusive band
a bold balance

the dry crack of kindling
two dead sparrows

white spiral of cloud on
the horizon

A Room in Oiron

Bald mouse
Bumblebee
          Hannibal
Sunflower Hare
Playing from cricket
the toes were like an organised spinet
                    Swallow
          Lout
Intelligence like lima coming out of the choruses
Phosphoric acid
Pantagruel leaves in peace
Pie
    field
nitrogen Loire
          Beat brides
chins like a pumpkin
Barefoot
Mole   Tambourine
                    Grang Gosier
The wind in Vienne bellows

Like Léa

In a
closed
off
square

a slow
set
light fade
to stage spot

along
the bench
a glance
enough

to seek
repetition

Take shelter in the wood it's a favourite place. Chop the lane back, branches scratch like machinery. Crater-like pot holes gather dust, then chaff then finally, water. To wake in such isolation offers comfort, emboldened by distant activity, and the field's daily cacophony. *For AC*

*

Morning phase under the clip dust has gathered second cup coffee steam what does it want with France? Read the 23 manifestos for an answer or maybe take a drop of Vladimir's tar with tape the line comes to life toward a new band in Liverpool in 1983 a 17 year old girl takes notes

*

Nightingale 6.09 a.m. *graceful chat alert song rich and fluty* musical murmurs before light Julian says enjoy the glow dark as comforter jam the signal Matt spots three on arrival in Berlin Taras Shevchenko points to such happiness 6.48 chorus joins in light hits the undergrowth

*

The Yellow Square on the D121 that was painted near to the four white dots in the summer of 2018 has faded twigs gather in ditches that are slowly being cleared the 99 cent blue gardening gloves are stowed under the stairs with the cans of WD-40 and the toolbox from Liverpool

Quest

I
Hovering around London
making frequent excursions

across the channel for long
walks over the hills of Boulogne

The Red Lion Inn at Stratford
sadly degenerated from excess of travel

17th June 'I think she be gone now Sir
May is the time to hear her'

the explanation is to be found in Shakespeare
who says 'the cuckoo is in June heard not regarded'

White limits the singing of the nightingale
until June 15 but seasons differ it can't be possible

that any class of feathered songsters
all stop on a given day

II
There is a tradition that when George I died
the nightingales all ceased singing for the year

out of grief at the sad event but he did not die
until June 21 that would give a margin of several days

for it seems that the nightingale ceases singing
the moment her brood is hatched after that event

you hear only a harsh chiding or anxious note
hence the poets who attribute her melancholy strains

to sorrow for the loss of her young are entirely at fault
but she probably does nothing of the kind

the song of a bird is not a reminiscence but an anticipation
and expresses happiness or joy only except in those cases

where the male bird having lost its mate sings for a few days
as if to call the lost one back

III
When the male renews his powers of song
after the young brood has been destroyed

or after it has flown away it is a sign that a new brood
is contemplated the song as it were the magic note

that calls the brood forth the poets therefore
in depicting the bird on such occasions as bewailing

the lost brood are wide of the mark
he is invoking and celebrating a new brood

encouraged by hearing that they were not done singing
yet they had often been heard during haying-time

opportunity to call them out with an imitator
the opening part of the song is called the 'challenge'

astonished at the strong piercing quality of the strain
it echoed in the woods and copses about

IV
The combination did not seem a likely place for nightingales
walking rapidly thitherward there were several warblers

but not Philomel probably missed the bird by just fifteen minutes
a broad well-kept path that seemed to have

the same inevitable right of way as a brook foxglove pierced
the lower foliage and wild growths everywhere its tall spires

of purple flowers the wild honeysuckle with a ranker and coarser
fragrance the situation began to look serious following

one of those inevitable footpaths that cuts diagonally through
the cemetery behind the old church the ear too critical

the editor had extended White's date of June 15 to July 1
as the time to which the nightingale continues in song

it is said they grow hoarse late in the season larks are seen
in buntings and a wren's song entrances like Philomel's

V
Startled by a quick brilliant call or whistle a few rods away that
            at once
recalled the imitator the long-sought bird was inflating her throat

how it had the quality that startles it pierced the gathering gloom
like a rocket the hermit thrush just tuning her instrument

Pause near other shrines not a sound the alternative
is to spend the night under the trees with the nightingales

and possibly surprise them at their revels in the small hours
of the morning or catch them at their matins

the prettiest little showers march across the country
in summer scarcely bigger that a street watering-cart

they keep the haymakers in perpetual flurry
the hay is got together inch by inch every inch is fought for

it is usually nearly worn out with handling
before the get it into the rick

VI
In Hitchin on the road between the station and the town
proper is Nightingale Lane famous for its songsters

it is understandable that this bird might keep people awake
at night by singing near their houses

there is something in the strain so startling
and awakening its start is a vivid flash of sound

here is the complete artist of whom all these other birds
are but hints and studies bright startling assured of great

compass and power it easily dominated all other notes
the harsher chur-r-r-rg notes serve as foil to her surpassing brilliancy

we have no bird-voice so piercing and loud with such flexibility
full-throated harmony and long-drawn cadences

though we have songs of more melody tenderness
and plaintiveness

Theolonius Monk

We always get the Nightingales we deserve —Ben Mandelson

Perhaps it is a desire
to confound
human expectation

Rhythmically consistent
long whistles
     then trills

& clicks shift
       & divergence

sometimes what we call
music is not the real music

Back in the start house
an invisible border
east transposes to west

unkempt green space
melodious
Sending Lady Load

even then out of kilter
a sequence at odds

Situate in soundscape
trees sound
like rolling waves

Some think the more
you know
the deeper the experience

Seek the unattainable
    the absent

the beautiful puzzle

Acknowledgements to David Rothenberg

A Nightingale

After Raymond Carver

A nightingale built a nest near the gate.
It was not R.F. Langley's nightingale.
Or Coleridge's. Or Keats', Arnold's or Milton's nightingale.
Or one of Shakespeare's nightingales, with its mazy
running soul of melancholy. This was our first nightingale.
Recorded for posterity, one early spring morning.
It also sang from a tall tree during daylight.
Tony said it was impossible.
But we saw it with our own eyes,
singing a variety of its 200 plus notes.

As you move through the world

Sort the merry
in myth ground
voluptuous hidden
leaf flower melancholy
magic air song

Summer's spot abroad
as happiest fame
nightingale in sunburst
Provençal immortal
thought unborn

C'est ma vérité

Allow the song to continue
to interrupt would only weaken the moment

end of summer morning chill
brings a refreshing air

as simple as broken silence
& the sun rising behind trees

What will humanity be without movement?

What is here relates to what is elsewhere
because what is elsewhere augments what is here

Regularity of the metronome embellished
piano *black white felt* sheet catching sail-like

evening sun shift with its angled shadows
& the reddening of tomatoes

these truths that cannot be categorised

Acknowledgements to Guillaume le Blanc

Acknowledgements

Some of the poems in this book have previously appeared in the following journals, sometimes in an alternate form:

A) Glimpse) of), Adjacent Pineapple, Ambit, Angry Old Man, Anthropocene, Bloom, Hobo Camp Review, Fried Chicken and Coffee, Full of Crow, The Goose, In Between Hangovers, In Other Words: Merida, International Times, The Journal, Litter, New Walk, The Ofi Press, Pages, Paratext, Poetry Salzburg Review, The Red Ceilings, Rusty Truck, Shearsman, Stride, Your One Phone Call, Zarf, zimZalla. My grateful thanks to the editors.

'C'est ma Vérité' was commissioned by Nottingham City of Literature for National Poetry Day 2019.

'Sycamore Street' was first published and recorded in connection with *Dial-a-Poem*, a multimedia community project supported by the AHRC and Nottingham Trent University (Nottingham, 2020).

'A Room in Oiron' uses text displayed in French and German by Lothar Baumgarten at Château Oiron, Oiron, France.

Every word in 'Quest' is drawn from 'A Hunt for the Nightingale' in *Fresh Fields* by John Burroughs (Cambridge, MA: The Riverside Press, 1896). There have been some slight edits. Thanks to John Seed.

Some poems have previously appeared in the following collections:

Liverpool Warehousing Co. Ltd. (Manchester: zimZalla, 2016); thanks to Tom Jenks.
Air Vault (Old Hunstanton: Oystercatcher, 2016); thanks to Peter Hughes.
The 140's (Nottingham: Leafe Press, 2018); thanks to Alan Baker.
Aire (New Mills: The Red Ceilings Press, 2018); thanks to Mark Cobley.
at first it felt like flying (with Charlie Baylis) (Beaworthy: Indigo Dreams Pamphlets, 2019); thanks to Ronnie Goodyer and Dawn Bauling.
The Lowdeine Chronicles, (with Nick Power) (Liverpool: erbacce-press, 2019); thanks to Alan Corkish.

Some of the poems have previously appeared in the following publications, sometimes in an alternate form. Thanks to the editors:

The Black Balloon (Nottingham: Launderette Books, 2015)
An Educated Desire: Robert Sheppard at 60 ed. Scott Thurston
    (Newton-Le Willows: Knives Forks and Spoons Press, 2015)
Face Down in the Book of Revelations: A Peter Hughes Festschrift (Old
    Hunstanton: Oystercatcher Press, 2016)
Monster (Nottingham: Launderette Books, 2016)
25 (Nottingham: Shoestring Books, 2019)

Some sources:

*Faith in the City: A Call for Action by Church and Nation. The Report
    of the Archbishop of Canterbury's Commission on Urban Priority
    Areas* (London: Church House Publishing, 1985)
Hans Arp from *Three Painter Poets* (Harmondsworth: Penguin, 1974)
*in*servitude exhibition at arc en rêve centre d'architecture, Bordeaux
Margaret Baker *Discovering the Folklore of Plants* (Aylesbury: Shire,
    1971)
Michael Head and The Strands *The Magical World of the Strands*
    (Megaphone Music, 1998)
Richard Mabey *The Book of the Nightingale* (London: Sinclair-
    Stevenson, 1997)
David Rothenberg *Nightingales in Berlin: Searching for the Perfect
    Sound* (Chicago, IL & London: Chicago University Press, 2019)
Ken Smith 'By the Northern Sea, a farewell to one woman' *The Poet
    Reclining* (Newcastle Upon Tyne: Bloodaxe Books, 1989)
Shack *H.M.S. Fable* (London Records, 1999)

Thanks to: Alan Baker, Alex Byron, Charlie Baylis, Tony Frazer, Linda Kemp, Nick Power, E.M. and W.J. Taylor, Nichola Taylor, Andrew Thacker, Rory Waterman, Cliff Yates, Tim Youngs, and all at Five Leaves Bookshop in Nottingham.